First edition published by Blended Mix Publishing
Contact: www.blendedmixpublishing.com

Copyright © 2023 Evika Kamille Belfon | All rights reserved

Copyright protects the voice of the author, encourages diversity of thought, creates space for uninhibited creativity, and adds value to the human experience. Thank you for buying this book and thereby promoting free speech. No portion of this book may be reproduced mechanically, electronically, or by any other means, including photocopy, without permission of the publisher or author except in the case of brief quotations embodied in critical articles and reviews. It is illegal to copy this book, post it to a website, or distribute by any other means without permission from the publisher or author.

The purpose of this book is to educate, inspire, and entertain as a work of creative nonfiction. The author and/or publisher shall have neither liability nor responsibility to anyone with respect to any loss or damage caused, or alleged to be caused, directly or indirectly by the information contained in this book.

Illustrated by Shehan Gunasekara
Author Photo: Meg Delagrange-Belfon
Cover Layout and Manuscript Formatting: Meg Delagrange-Belfon

PRINTED IN THE UNITED STATES OF AMERICA

ILLUSTRATED BY SHEHAN GUNASEKARA

THE MAGIC OF EMOTIONS

EVIKA BELFON

My name is

_____

and my feelings matter!

You can feel excited...

You can feel calm...

...but respected.

You can feel anxious...

You can feel a LOT of emotions at the same time.

Don't feel bad about feeling! Just be you.

Every feeling you have is like a unique piece of a big puzzle, and it's okay to feel them all!

A Feel Wheel

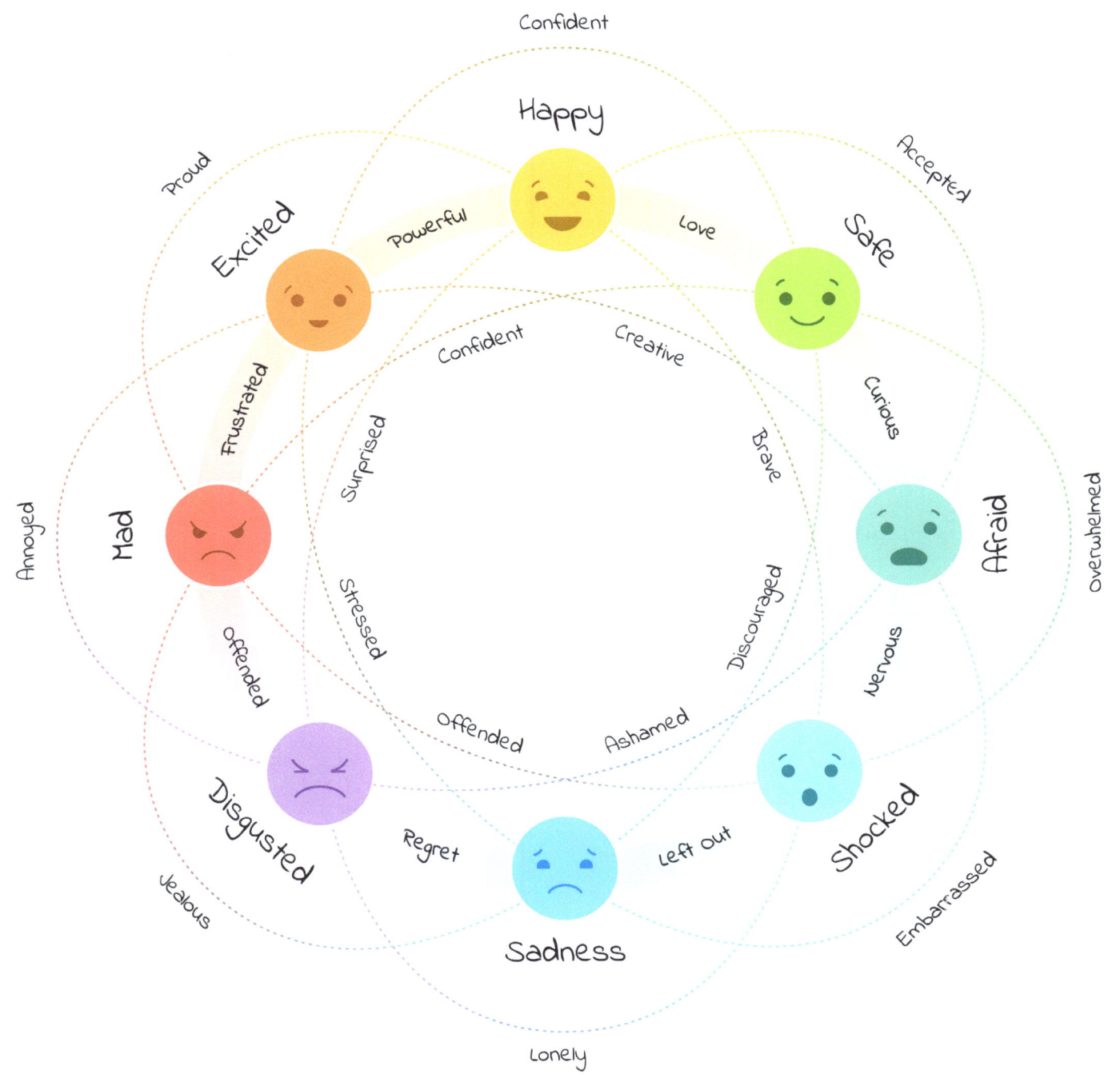

Use the feel wheel to help you find your emotion.

Emotions Are Not "Bad"

Some emotions feel comfortable and some emotions feel uncomfortable. But, there's no such thing as a "bad" emotion.

Sometimes you may feel angry. Other times you may feel scared. You can also feel both scared AND angry at the same time!

You can feel many different emotions at the same time and that's okay!

Coping with Emotions

There are different ways to cope with your emotions, especially when they feel really big!
This is a guide to help you with your feelings.

➤ Talk about your feelings.
When you're happy, excited, or even sad, angry, and afraid, find a trusted grown-up, like a parent or teacher, to talk to. They can help you understand your emotions and help you feel better.

➤ Use your words.
Sometimes, when you're upset, it helps to use words to explain how you feel. Say things like, "I'm mad because..." or "I'm sad because..." This helps others understand what's going on inside of you.

➢ Take a deep breath.
When you feel really angry, scared, or nervous, take a deep breath. Pretend you're smelling a flower (breathe in) and then blow out the candles on a birthday cake (breathe out slowly). This can help you feel calmer.

➢ Draw, write, or scribble!
Get some paper and colorful crayons or markers. Draw, write, or scribble how you're feeling. You can make a happy picture when you're happy or a sad picture when you're sad.

➢ Take a break.
If you're feeling overwhelmed or upset, it's okay to take a break. Find a quiet place to sit or lie down, close your eyes, and take some deep breaths. Think of a happy place or something you like. This helps you feel more in control.

➢ Ask for a hug.
When you're feeling down or upset, ask for a hug from someone you trust. Hugs can make you feel loved and safe. Sometimes, a big hug is all you need to feel better.

You are magical.

Evika Belfon

Meet the Author

Hey there! My name is Evika Belfon, and I'm a Caribbean-American magical black girl! When I was eight, I wrote this book. My mission in life is to help other kids from all around the world embrace and celebrate their own unique blend of emotions.

When I'm not writing, you can usually find me hanging out with my family or having playdates with my friends. I also have a big thing for unicorns (who doesn't?!), yummy foods, daydreaming, and interior decorating.

Through my book, I hope to inspire you to be proud of who you are. We all have something magical inside of us, so go ahead and celebrate the way you feel! You belong here with all your magical mixed up emotions!

A GUIDE FOR PARENTS
5 Questions to Ask Your Child

How are you feeling?
Asking your child how they are feeling can open up a conversation about their emotions and help them feel comfortable expressing themselves.

What made you smile today?
Asking your child about positive experiences can help them recognize and acknowledge positive emotions.

What made you sad or upset today?
Asking your child about negative experiences can help them process their emotions.

How did you feel when (specific event) happened?
Asking your child about a specific event can help them understand their emotions and why they are feeling a certain way.

What can we do to help you feel better?
Asking your child how you can help them cope with their emotions can help them feel supported and understood. It can also provide an opportunity to teach them healthy coping mechanisms.

Do you know a young author with a story to tell?
We can help you publish their book!

Scan the QR code with your phone to learn more
or visit www.blendedmixpublishing.com

AT BLENDED MIX PUBLISHING, we are dedicated to empowering authors by offering a range of personalized services that cater to their unique needs. Our founders, Kelvin Belfon, a pastor and educational speaker, and Meg Belfon, a successful entrepreneur, combine their spiritual leadership and creative expertise to guide our vision. Our blended, interracial family is the heart of our inspiration. We are strong advocates for personal growth, social change, and family unity, reflected in our dedication to authors who share these values.

Learn more at www.blendedmixpublishing.com

www.ingramcontent.com/pod-product-compliance
Lightning Source LLC
Chambersburg PA
CBHW041423010526
44119CB00015B/351